*This book was a gift
to our library
from Capstone Press.*

Oceans

by Susan H. Gray

Content Adviser: Terrence E. Young Jr., M.Ed., M.L.S.,
Jefferson Parish (La.) Public Schools

Reading Adviser: Dr. Linda D. Labbo,
Department of Reading Education, College of Education,
The University of Georgia

COMPASS POINT BOOKS

Minneapolis, Minnesota

FIRST REPORTS

Compass Point Books
3109 West 50th Street, #115
Minneapolis, MN 55410

Visit Compass Point Books on the Internet at *www.compasspointbooks.com*
or e-mail your request to *custserv@compasspointbooks.com*

Photographs ©: Jeff Divine/FPG International, cover; North Wind Picture Archives, 4; Norbert Wu, 5; Tsado/Tom Stack and Associates, 7; International Stock/Ronn Maretea, 9; NASA, 11; International Stock/Robert Brown, 13; Index Stock Imagery, 15; Visuals Unlimited/Peter K. Ziminski, 16 top and bottom;Telegraph Colour Library/FPG International, 17; Norbert Wu, 18; Visuals Unlimited/Jeanette Thomas, 19; Visuals Unlimited, 20–21; Index Stock Imagery, 22; James P. Rowan, 23 top and bottom; Norbert Wu, 25; Tom and Therisa Stack/Tom Stack and Associates, 26; Visuals Unlimited/Whoi D. Foster, 27, 28; JPL/Tsado/Tom Stack and Associates, 30; Index Stock Imagery, 31 top; International Stock/Beverly Factor, 31 bottom; Visuals Unlimited/David Fleetham, 32; International Stock/Ron Sanford, 33 top; International Stock/Miwako Ikeda, 33 bottom; Peter Parks/Mo Yung Productions, 34 top and bottom; Visuals Unlimited/Hal Beral, 35 top; David and Tess Young/Tom Stack and Associates, 35 bottom; Visuals Unlimited/David Fleetham, 36; Michael Nolan/ Tom Stack and Associates, 37 top; David Fleetham/FPG International, 37 bottom; Brian Parker/Tom Stack and Associates, 38; Dave B. Fleetham/Tom Stack and Associates, 39; Visuals Unlimited/John S. Lough, 40; International Stock/Mark Newman, 41; Index Stock Imagery, 42; Photo Network/Jim Schwabel, 43.

Editors: E. Russell Primm and Emily J. Dolbear
Photo Researcher: Svetlana Zhurkina
Photo Selector: Dawn Friedman
Design: Bradfordesign, Inc.

Library of Congress Cataloging-in-Publication Data
Gray, Susan Heinrichs.
    Oceans / by Susan H. Gray.
        p. cm. — (First reports)
    Includes bibliographical references and index.
    Summary: An introduction to the oceans, describing the topography of the ocean floor, plants and animals that live there, and threats to the biome.
    ISBN 0-7565-0022-2 (hardcover : lib. bdg.)
    ISBN 0-7565-0943-2 (paperback)
    1. Ocean—Juvenile literature. [1. Ocean.] I. Title. II. Series.
    551.46—dc21
    577.5'3—dc21   00-008532

Table of Contents

Ocean Explorers

Hundreds of years ago, people were afraid to sail far out on the oceans. Some thought that sea monsters would swallow their boats. Others thought their ships would drop off the edge of the world.

Then brave sailors began going farther and farther away from land. They didn't tumble off the edge of the Earth. Instead, they found lands and people

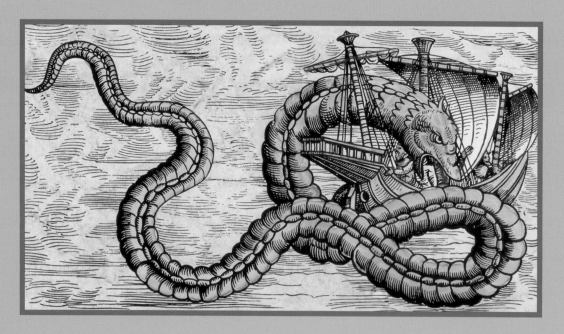

▲ An imaginary sea serpent, from 1555

▲ *An underwater vessel piloted by its inventor, Graeme Hawke.*

they had never heard of. They saw amazing new
plants and animals. They made discovery after
discovery.

Today, explorers go deep down in the oceans. Others sail into the coldest waters to learn new things. These explorers have plenty of work to do. After all, oceans cover almost three-fourths of the world.

How Many Oceans Are There?

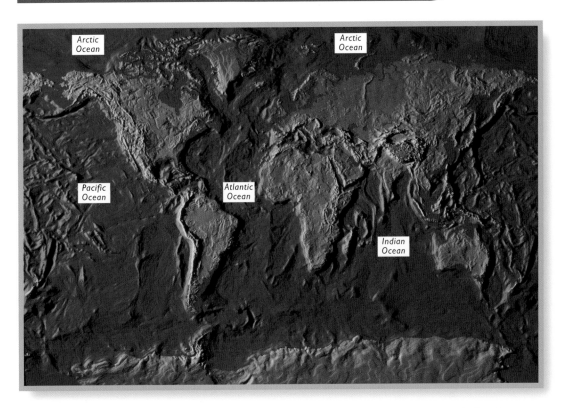

Arctic Ocean

Arctic Ocean

Pacific Ocean

Atlantic Ocean

Indian Ocean

▲ Earth's oceans

Earth has four oceans. The largest of these is the Pacific Ocean. It lies all along the western border of North and South America and the eastern side of Asia. It is so huge that all but one of the continents border on it. The next biggest is the Atlantic Ocean.

It lies along the eastern border of North and South America and the western side of Europe and Africa.

The third-biggest ocean is the Indian Ocean. The Indian Ocean is bordered by Australia and Indonesia on the east, Africa on the west, Asia on the north, and Antarctica on the south.

The Arctic Ocean is the world's smallest ocean. It lies to the north. There are some scientists who say that there is a fifth ocean—the Antarctic. The Antarctic Ocean surrounds the South Pole.

Iceberg!

▲ An iceberg in the Antarctic Ocean

Huge mountains of floating ice called **icebergs** are found in the Arctic and Antarctic Oceans. Only the very tip of an iceberg can be seen. Most of the iceberg is hidden underwater.

In 1913, several countries formed the International Ice Patrol to watch for icebergs and warn sailors. At first, the patrol used ships to search the North Atlantic for icebergs. Now they fly airplanes over the ocean to spot icebergs. Then they give the information to ships in the area.

What's in the Ocean?

▲ *View from space of river deposits in the ocean*

The oceans are all connected and they are alike in many ways. All oceans have salt and minerals in their water. They also have other materials such as chlorine, sulfur, and calcium. When rivers and streams flow over land, they pick up all these substances. When the rivers reach the ocean, these materials pour into the seawater.

The rivers and streams even pick up bits of gold along the way. Billions of dollars in tiny gold specks are floating in the oceans. Unfortunately, it costs too much to filter out these small bits of gold.

Always on the Move

▲ *A crashing wave*

Ocean waters are always moving. They move in three main ways—by **waves**, **currents**, and **tides**. When wind whips across the ocean waters, it causes waves. The strongest winds cause the highest waves.

Currents are movements of large sections of ocean water, like rivers in the sea. The wind pushes along these huge sections. The levels of salt and heat in the water and Earth's rotation affect currents.

In the northern half of the world, currents flow in the same direction as the hands of a clock, or clockwise. In the southern half of the world, they move in the opposite direction from the hands of a clock, or counterclockwise. The Pacific, Atlantic, and Indian currents all meet at the Antarctic Ocean. Here, the water flows counterclockwise around the South Pole.

Ship captains know where all the currents are. Sometimes they steer their ships right into currents and let the waters carry them along. This way, the ships use less energy and sail faster.

Tides are very slow movements of the whole ocean. The rise and fall of the tides are caused by the attraction of the moon and the sun. Every day, the forces of gravity on the sun and moon slowly draw the

▲ *The tide on a beach*

water higher and higher on Earth. Then they pull it back down again. The movement is almost too slow to see. It takes about twelve hours.

▼ Low tide

▲ High tide

From Shore to Ocean Floor

▲ *Waves crashing on the rocky shore of Cornwall, England*

The place where the ocean touches the land is called the **shore**. The land that slants down from the shore into the ocean and keeps slanting down for miles is called the **continental shelf**.

17

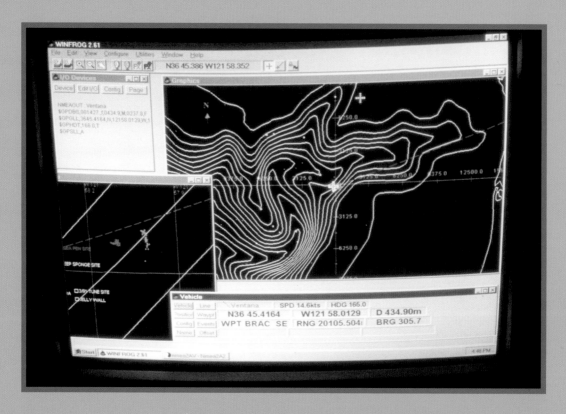

▲ *A sonar screen shows an underwater canyon near Monterey, California.*

Farther out in the ocean, the slanting land gets very steep. This is the **continental slope**. Finally, the land stops slanting down. This is called the **ocean floor**.

At one time, people thought the ocean floor was flat. Then scientists on ships began using sound waves to check the ocean floor. They sent sound waves down to the ocean floor and waited for them to bounce back. Some sounds returned quickly. Other sounds took longer to return. These sounds had to travel a long way to the ocean floor and back. This use of sound is called **sonar**. Sonar showed us that the ocean floor has many peaks and valleys.

▲ *A scientist using a sonar machine*

Using sonar, it would have taken more than 100 years to check out the whole ocean floor. So scientists decided to try something else. They sent special cameras and film up into space. The cameras took pictures of the oceans that showed high and low places on the ocean floor. The pictures came back to Earth and showed some surprising things.

The pictures showed 40,000 miles (64,360 kilometers) of mountain chains, or ridges, on the

▲ *The island of Hawaii, as seen from space*

ocean floor. They run through every ocean. The tallest mountain chains are in the Pacific Ocean.

Some of these underwater mountains are volcanoes. They shoot lava right into the water. Over many years, they grow taller and taller. Some even rise above the water's surface. The islands of Hawaii, the Philippines, and Iceland were formed in this way.

▲ *Lava pouring into the sea*

▼ *Lava fields in Iceland*　　　　　　　　　▲ *Cones formed by volcanic lava in Hawaii*

Where Is the Deepest Place on Earth?

The ocean floor also has huge, deep cracks called **trenches**. The most famous one is the Mariana Trench in the Pacific Ocean. In 1960, two men planned to go all the way down into the trench. One morning, they got cameras—and some candy bars—and climbed into a special deep-sea vessel called a bathyscaphe. The men closed the door and slowly went down to the bottom of the ocean.

When they were almost 1 mile (1.6 kilometer) down, the bathyscaphe sprang a leak. The men were scared, but they kept on going. Soon the leak stopped. When the bathyscaphe finally settled on the ocean floor, it was 7 miles (11 kilometers) down. They had reached the deepest place on Earth.

The men flipped on a light outside the bathy-scaphe and looked around the trench. They were sure

▲ *Clams, crabs, and worms live deep on the ocean floor.*

it was too dark and cold and deep for living things. But suddenly a fish swam by! They took its picture before coming back up.

▲ *The Aquarius 2000 Habitat, a deep-sea exploring vessel*

What Are Chimneys?

▲ *Smokers are chimneys that shoot out chemicals.*

Since then, many amazing things have been found on the ocean floor. In 1977, scientists found holes where very hot water bubbles up. Sometimes hot water spills out of structures called chimneys. Chimneys can be as tall as a four-story building. Some chimneys

▲ *Giant tube worms on the ocean floor*

spew chemicals that turn the water black. They are called black smokers. Others shoot out milky white chemicals. They are called white smokers. The liquid from the chimneys can be hotter than 800° Fahrenheit (427° Celsius). More than eighty chimneys have been found in the Atlantic and Pacific Oceans.

About 300 kinds of animals live near these chimneys. There are giant clams 1 foot (30 centimeters) wide, and bright-red gigantic worms measuring 12 feet (4 meters) long! They live in tubes that stick up from the ocean floor. These animals are not found anywhere else in the world.

Life in the Ocean

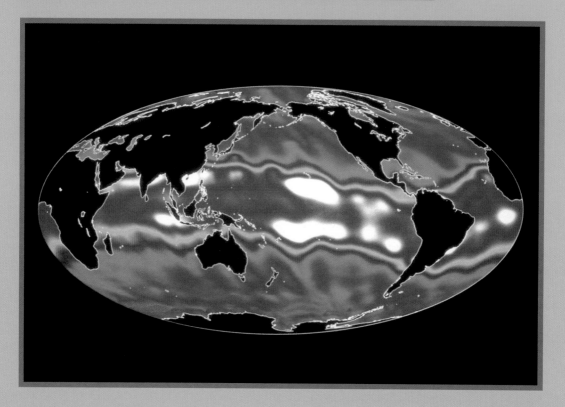

▲ *A map showing ocean temperatures*

Plants and animals live in the warmest and the coldest oceans. In warm, shallow tropical seas, tiny, soft animals called polyps build coral reefs out of their crusty little cup skeletons. After many years, millions of polyps form a huge structure. All kinds of sharks,

◄ An aerial view of the
Great Barrier Reef in
Australia

Polyps in a
coral reef ▶

▲ *A whitetip reef shark*

starfish, crabs, snails, and slugs live around coral reefs.

Cold waters have animals too. The animals that live in the Arctic and Antarctic Oceans usually have round bodies that store lots of fat. This helps keep them warm. Walruses live in Arctic areas. Penguins swim in the Antarctic Ocean. Seals live in both places.

▼ Adelie penguins   ▲ Bull walruses

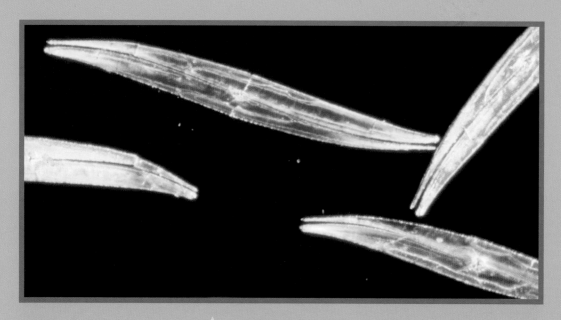

Phytoplankton are tiny plants that live in the ocean's upper layer.

In the open ocean, most plants and animals live in the upper layer of the water. The sun shines on this layer and helps plants to grow. Many plants are too tiny to be seen. Other plants, such as the large and leafy kelp, can stretch out 200 feet (61 meters) long.

Tiny animals called zooplankton also live in the upper layer. Some whales and many kinds of fish eat zooplankton.

▲ Giant kelp

◄ Zooplankton

Many kinds of animals live in the open ocean. Tuna and stinging jellyfish swim in the upper waters. Whale sharks 50 feet (15 meters) long lie very still and suck in plankton. Dolphins and whales glide through the water and come up for air.

▲ *Southern bluefin tuna swimming near South Australia*

▼ Bottle-nose dolphins in the Pacific Ocean   ▲ A humpback whale comes up for air

▲ A jellyfish, or sea nettle

Deeper in the ocean, there is very little sunlight. Here, about two-thirds of the animals make their own light. This is called **bioluminescence**. Some fish wiggle lighted body parts. Smaller fish are drawn to the bright lights—and they are quickly eaten. Squid live in the deep sea and squirt bioluminescent ink on their enemies.

Sunlight cannot reach the deep ocean floor. Some animals there creep slowly through the icy water. Others stay on the ocean floor all their lives. These bottom animals eat one another or anything else that drifts down to them.

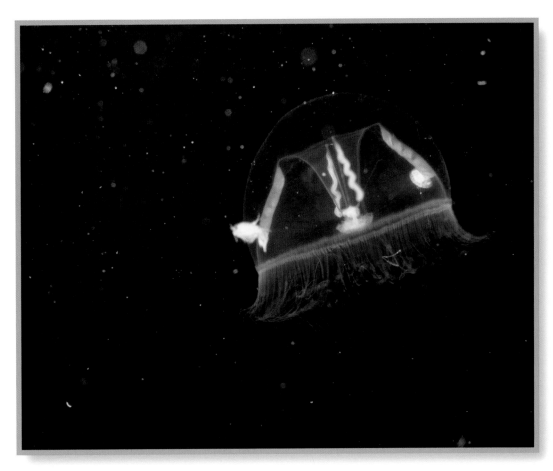

▲ *A jellyfish displaying bioluminescence*

What Pollutes the Ocean?

Sometimes poisons drift down to the ocean floor. They can come from several places. Cities on land dump sewage and factory wastes into the water. Cruise ships sometimes throw garbage overboard. Tankers can leak oil.

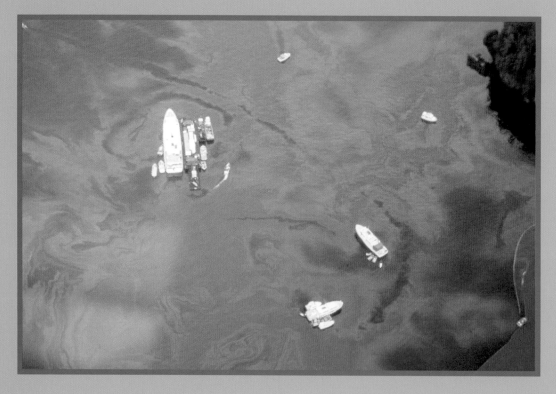

▲ *Cleaning up after the Exxon Valdez oil spill*

▲ *A bird covered with oil after the spill*

In 1989, an oil tanker called the *Exxon Valdez* struck a reef in Alaska. More than 10 million gallons (38 million liters) of oil covered hundreds of miles of water. Thousands of birds, otters, and other animals died. People spent years trying to clean up the mess.

In 1999, the number of bald eagles began to return to normal in the area. But harbor seals and other animals were still few in number. In many places, the oil has remained in the rocks and the ground. It will be there for years.

People today know more than the ancient sailors about Earth's waters. Now we know that we don't

▲ *A submarine exploring the waters of Micronesia*

▲ *The Atlantic Ocean near Bermuda*

need to fear oceans and the plants and animals that live there. Instead, we need to continue to recognize their value. All of life depends on the oceans. We must find ways to protect them.

Glossary

bioluminescence—the light that an animal gives off

continental shelf—the land that slants down from the shore into the ocean for miles

continental slope—the very steep slope in the ocean beyond the continental shelf

currents—movements of large sections of the ocean, like rivers in the sea

icebergs—huge mountains of floating ice

ocean floor—the bottom of the ocean

shore—the point where the ocean touches land

sonar—the use of sound for locating objects

tides—the rise and fall of the ocean every twelve hours, caused by the gravitational pull of the moon and the sun

trenches—huge, deep cracks on the ocean floor

waves—moving ridges of ocean water caused by wind

Did You Know?

- About 2.5 percent of seawater consists of salt.

- A powerful wave caused by an earthquake is called a tsunami. It can move at the speed of 600 miles (965 kilometers) per hour.

- The Pacific Ocean covers one-third of Earth's surface. That's about 70 million square miles (181 million square kilometers).

- If the Greenland and Antarctic icecaps melted, the oceans of the world would rise about 200 feet (61 meters).

At a Glance

Locations: Pacific Ocean (western border of North America); Atlantic Ocean (eastern border of North America); Arctic Ocean (north of most of Asia, Europe, and North America); Indian Ocean (bordered by Africa, Asia, Indonesia, Australia, and Antarctica)

Description: Body of saltwater that covers almost three-fourths of Earth

Common animals: Coral polyps, sharks, starfish, walruses, penguins, seals, squid, jellyfish, fish

Common plants: Kelp, algae

Want to Know More?

At the Library

Mariner, Tom. *Oceans*. New York: M. Cavendish, 1990.

Nye, Bill, and Ian G. Saunders. *Bill Nye the Science Guy's Big Blue Ocean*. New York: Hyperion Books for Children, 1999.

Pechter, Alese. *What's in the Deep?: An Underwater Adventure for Children*. Washington, D.C.: Acropolis Books, 1991.

Wells, Susan. *Explore the World of Mighty Oceans*. New York: Golden Books, 1992.

On the Web

For more information on *Oceans*, use FactHound to track down Web sites related to this book.

1. Go to *www.facthound.com*
2. Type in a search word related to this book or this book ID: 0756500222.
3. Click on the *Fetch It* button.

Your trusty FactHound will fetch the best Web sites for you!

On the Road

Monterey Bay Aquarium
886 Cannery Row
Monterey, CA 93940-1085
831/648-4800
To see a wide variety of marine mammals up close

Index

About the Author

Susan H. Gray holds bachelor's and master's degrees in zoology from the University of Arkansas in Fayetteville. She has taught classes in general biology, human anatomy, and physiology. She has also worked as a freshwater biologist and scientific illustrator. In her twenty years as a writer, Susan H. Gray has covered many topics and written a variety of science books for children.